mecca

by the same author

THE FOURSOME
ALPHA BETA
THE SEA ANCHOR
OLD FLAMES

mecca

TED WHITEHEAD

FABER & FABER
3 Queen Square
London

First published in 1977
by Faber and Faber Limited
3 Queen Square London WC1
Printed in Great Britain by
Whitstable Litho Whitstable
All rights reserved

ISBN 0 571 10981 0

All rights whatsoever in this play are strictly
reserved and applications for permission to perform
it, etc. must be made in advance, before rehearsals
begin, to Margaret Ramsay Ltd, 14a Goodwin's Court,
St Martin's Lane, London WC2

Conditions of Sale

This book is sold subject to the condition that it shall
not, by way of trade or otherwise, be lent, re-sold,
hired out or otherwise circulated without the publisher's
prior consent in any form of binding or cover other than
that in which it is published and without a similar
condition including this condition being imposed on the
subsequent purchaser

© 1977 by Ted Whitehead

CHARACTERS

in order of appearance

SANDY	a girl of about twenty
ANDREW	late-forties
JILL	thirty-eight
EUNICE	about forty
IAN	mid-twenties
MARTIN	thirty-nine
BOY	an Arab in his teens
AHMED	an Arab in his late twenties

Scene

The action takes place during the course of a day at a holiday village on the Atlantic coast of Morocco

ACT ONE

Scene 1

A suntrap: a garden bounded by a white stone wall, about six foot high, topped with broken glass and railings wrapped with barbed wire. In the centre of the wall at the back is a double gate, made of wood and bolted at top and bottom.
Left, an area of garden with palms and exotic plants and flowers. A swing hangs from a tree. There is an ornamental fountain in blue and orange tile.
Right, a paved area leading to a swimming pool (off). On the paving a giant draughts set is laid out. Against the wall, a stack of foam mattresses, and a number of plastic moulds in various colours on which the mattresses can be laid.
The village is located on the outskirts of a small Moroccan town. In the distance we see, stretching off, a blaze of white houses dominated by a steep pink minaret and the brown hulk of the Casbah. In the foreground, an expanse of sand and trees.
The sky is an intense blue and the sun burns down. The time is mid-morning.
SANDY sits on the swing, reading from a primer in colloquial Arabic. She's a slender girl with blonde shoulder-length hair and wears a bikini.

SANDY: *(Reads)* 'Ya bi nt, enti keslane ketir.' Bint? *(Reads)* 'Girl, you are very idle.' *(Little girl's voice)* 'La, ya sidi, manish keslan! 'No, sir, I am not idle!'

(ANDREW comes on.)

ANDREW: Who isn't idle?

SANDY: 'Neharkum sa'id.'

ANDREW: What?

SANDY: 'May your day be prosperous.'

ANDREW: It's prospering now.

SANDY: You're supposed to reply: 'May your day be prosperous and *blessed*.'

ANDREW: Neharkum sa'id whatever it was ... to you.

SANDY: That puts you one up on me, see.

ANDREW: I see.

SANDY: And you're supposed to peer into my eyes to show you really mean it.

ANDREW: *(Peers)* Like this.

SANDY: Now mine's prospering too!

(SANDY turns over the pages.

ANDREW smiles at her. He's a solid-looking man in his forties, wearing a white shirt, fawn trousers and cap. He carries a bottle of red wine. He puts this down and pulls a mattress from the stack, and lays it alongside Sandy's mattress, which is strewn with her things. Strips down to swimming trunks. Distant sound of Moroccan music on the radio.

ANDREW opens the bottle of wine.)

ANDREW: Like a glass?

SANDY: I'll just have a sip of yours.

(ANDREW pours a glass of wine, gives it to Sandy, who sips.

ANDREW looks around, then up at the sky, luxuriating.)

ANDREW: Two weeks of this makes the other fifty bearable.

SANDY: *(Laughing)* Christ, who writes these things?

ANDREW: What?

SANDY: *(Reads)* 'Nimarek huwa qawi giddan, we-himart huwa qawi keman.'

ANDREW: What's that?

SANDY: 'Your ass is very sturdy and my ass is sturdy also.

ANDREW: Is that an English or an American ass?

SANDY: I think it's a four-legged ass.

ANDREW: Over here you've got to be careful.

(As SANDY sips the wine, ANDREW takes hold of the rope of the swing and pushes and pulls. The swing moves at first slowly then faster and higher. SANDY laughs, hangs on to the rope and balances the glass of wine. Finally ANDREW catches hold of the seat and stops the swing. SANDY slips off and the wine shoots over ANDREW.)

SANDY: Ooops! Sorry!

ANDREW: My fault.

(SANDY picks up a towel and wipes ANDREW's chest.)

Thanks.

(ANDREW refills the glass. SANDY looks through a pair of binoculars into the auditorium. Climbs up on the fountain to get a better look.)

SANDY: Pretty little town, isn't it?

ANDREW: At this distance.

SANDY: Have you been in?

ANDREW: We had a look around.

SANDY: It looks really picturesque.

ANDREW: It is, in its way ...

SANDY: I was thinking of going in this afternoon.

ANDREW: What? On your own?

SANDY: With my primer.

ANDREW: I wouldn't advise it.

SANDY: Oh, why?

ANDREW: They're not used to tourists here ... well, particularly not somebody looking like you.

SANDY: I'll be wearing my jeans.

ANDREW: *(Laughs)* No ... I mean, they even stare at me in the streets, but ...

SANDY: I'll have to buy a yashmak.

ANDREW: They do have a different attitude to women here.
(Silence)

SANDY: That's a pity. Half the fun is in just taking off and following your nose and seeing where you end up.

ANDREW: Yes ... *(Pause)* It's certainly worth a visit. Up there on top of the hill there's a café in an orange grove overlooking the Atlantic.

SANDY: Up at the top?

ANDREW: Yes ... in the town.

SANDY: Fantastic!

ANDREW: If you're keen ... I wouldn't mind going over again.

SANDY: Are you sure?

ANDREW: Yes.

SANDY: I'd love to see it.

ANDREW: I'll ask Eunice.

(ANDREW lifts SANDY down from the fountain. As he does so, JILL comes on.)

JILL: Morning campers!

(ANDREW swings around.)

Don't worry, it's only me.

ANDREW: How are you this morning?

JILL: Epic. Absolutely epic!

(JILL is a sensuous-looking woman in her thirties with vivid red hair, wearing a short kaftan and carrying a

beachbag and a bottle of wine. She looks around for the best spot to sun-bathe, then pulls down a mattress and arranges her things on it. Slips out of the kaftan, under which she wears a tiny bikini. Opens her bottle of wine, pours a glass, and sits, drinking.)

JILL: Ahh.

ANDREW: How's Martin?

JILL: Martin?

ANDREW: Is he all right this morning?

JILL: As all right as ever ... why?

ANDREW: He came hammering on the door of our chalet last night ... it must have been about three o'clock in the morning, I think. I got up and opened the door and he was standing there with blood pouring down his face. It was a nasty cut. I think it could have done with a stitch really ... but anyway I cleaned it up and put some iodine on and a plaster.

JILL: I hope you charged him a fee.

ANDREW: D'you know how he did it?

JILL: He ... when I got back from the disco he was in bed snoring. He'd been out on the town.

ANDREW: He seemed pretty sloshed.

JILL: I was pretty sloshed myself. *(Stands)* What's the water like?

SANDY: Super.

(JILL goes off to the pool.)

ANDREW: See what you're letting yourself in for?

SANDY: What?

ANDREW: Once you're a doctor you're never off duty.

SANDY: I think I'll keep it a secret.

ANDREW: You can't really.

SANDY: I don't even know whether I want to be a doctor. *(Pause)* I suppose that sounds like heresy to you?

ANDREW: *(Smiles)* It's not everyone's vocation.

SANDY: No, but after two years' studying ...

ANDREW: What made you choose medicine?

SANDY: When I was a girl I was obsessed with Florence Nightingale. I wanted to be like her. I had visions of myself bandaging handsome heroes in field hospitals. Huh!

ANDREW: But you changed ...

SANDY: Yes, in my teens I decided I wanted to be a neuro-surgeon ... you know ... dedicated *and* rich.

ANDREW: And what now?

SANDY: What?

ANDREW: What do you want to do now?

SANDY: That's the trouble ... I don't know. I could see myself working with the volunteer services in Asia or Africa ... you know. But I'm not sure whether that isn't another ego trip. Another pipe dream!

ANDREW: I don't see why it should be ...

SANDY: I'm not knocking these services.

ANDREW: Then what?

SANDY: I just couldn't trust my own motives. I wouldn't know if I was being idealistic ... or irresponsible ... or both. I suspect that Florence is still lurking somewhere inside me.

(EUNICE comes on. She's an attractive but tense-looking woman, wearing a blouse and skirt.)

EUNICE: Darling ... did you hear about the tours?

ANDREW: The tours?

EUNICE: Yes, there are two, going off this morning ... in a few minutes, actually. If we dash we could just catch them.

ANDREW: Where are they going?

EUNICE: There's one to Agadir and one to Marrakesh.

ANDREW: Do you want to go?

EUNICE: Don't you?

ANDREW: I don't know ...

EUNICE: It's just that ... well, you did say you were looking forward to seeing something of the country, and ...

ANDREW: Yes ... yes.

EUNICE: They're going in a few minutes.

(ANDREW looks at SANDY.)

Ahmed was saying that the tour of Marrakesh is really fascinating. You know, snake-charmers, sword-swallowers, fire-eaters ... and apparently it's all quite authentic.

ANDREW: *(To SANDY)* Do you fancy going?

SANDY: I'd love to -

ANDREW: Would you?

SANDY: But not today. I want to see the town first.

ANDREW: *(To EUNICE)* We were thinking we might go and have a look around the town.

EUNICE: Again?

ANDREW: You liked the café in the orange grove, didn't you?

EUNICE: I liked *that*.

ANDREW: I thought we might show it to Sandy.

EUNICE: But I'm not wild about going into the town again.

ANDREW: Oh ...

SANDY: I'll manage all right.

ANDREW: No ...

EUNICE: *(To ANDREW)* You definitely don't want to go on the tour?

ANDREW: You don't mind, do you?

EUNICE: No ... I just thought you wanted to.

ANDREW: We can go on the next one.

EUNICE: All right ... as you like.

(Pause. EUNICE sits on the edge of the mattress.)

ANDREW: Would you like a drink?

EUNICE: I can't drink in this heat.

(JILL comes back from the pool.)

JILL: Phew! It's cold when you come out.

(JILL rubs herself vigorously with a towel.)

ANDREW: Like a glass of wine?

JILL: Thanks.

(ANDREW pours a glass for JILL.)

ANDREW: Sandy?

SANDY: Could I just have a sip of yours?

ANDREW: Of course.

(SANDY sips ANDREW's drink, then sits on the swing as before, reading the Arabic primer.)

SANDY: *(Laughs)* Here's one for you, Andrew.

ANDREW: What?

SANDY: *(Reads)* 'El-hakim da huwa meshgul qawi? La, huwa keslan ketir.'

ANDREW: What's that?

SANDY: 'Is this doctor very busy? No, he is very indolent.'

ANDREW: *(Laughing)* This here doctor is going to be very indolent from now on!

SANDY: Jesus!

ANDREW: What?

SANDY: *(Reads)* 'El-yehudi dik huwa ol-qonsul el-nimsawi.' Which means: 'That Jew is the German Consul.'

ANDREW: That's a handy phrase to know.

SANDY: It's too much! *(SANDY laughs, slips off the swing.)* Think I'll have a dip. Cool off.

ANDREW: Yes ... it's a scorcher, isn't it?

(SANDY goes off to the pool.)

16

(To EUNICE) Have you got your costume on?

EUNICE: No.

ANDREW: Go and get it ...

EUNICE: What?

ANDREW: We'll have a swim.

EUNICE: I don't want to.

ANDREW: Why not?

EUNICE: I'm not in the mood. You have a swim.

(ANDREW sits down.)

Oh for God's sake ...

ANDREW: What?

EUNICE: Go and have a swim.

(ANDREW goes off to the pool.

JILL puts on sunglasses and lies back.)

Why does that girl always insist on having a sip of somebody else's wine, or a drag of somebody else's cigarette, rather than having one of her own?

JILL: It's cheaper.

EUNICE: Oh, is that it?

JILL: No, but ... she does share *her* things too.

EUNICE: Yes ... at dinner she's forever picking bits off other people's plates and offering bits off her plate. Maybe I'm too fastidious, but –

JILL: I don't mind that ...

EUNICE: What?

JILL: She gives me all her meat.

EUNICE: She's vegetarian.

JILL: She shares everything.

EUNICE: 'Everything'?

JILL: Sharing is the latest fashion with her generation, actually I envy her like hell.

EUNICE: Do you?

JILL: Yes, I do.

EUNICE: Why?

JILL: She seems so free and easy and full of life.

EUNICE: She'll get over it.

JILL: What she reminds me of ... is those girls you see prancing up and down the King's Road in faded jeans with tight little arses and bobbing tits.

EUNICE: It's only a phase.

JILL: Is it?

EUNICE: You can't prance and bob when you're pushing a pram.

JILL: So you carry your baby on your back, Indian-style.

EUNICE: That's all right as long as you're young.

JILL: But they *stay* young.

EUNICE: Really?

JILL: I mean they don't go hurtling into middle age as soon as they get married or have kids, like our lot. I mean your generation ... and mine. Admit it, Eunice. We were taught to spend our youth trying to look mature and our maturity trying to look young. We were terrified of being left on the shelf. Our lot were *obsessed* with sex ... well, sex and babies. Christ, the number of times I've heard women - yes, women - discussing some poor demented female who's going mad with neglect and frustration, and then saying: 'What she needs is a husband', or 'What she needs is a baby'.

EUNICE: But it's often true ...

JILL: That's the saddest thing of all!

EUNICE: But can you really say that when you haven't had any children?

JILL: Oh, Christ, not that one ...

EUNICE: What?

JILL: You mean I've got to have children to find out I

don't want them?

EUNICE: You might change your mind ...

JILL: I might change my sex. *(Pause)* I do think that Sandy is an entirely new breed ... a kind of twentieth-century virgin.

EUNICE: Virgin?

JILL: Nothing to do with the hymen.

(IAN comes on. He's a powerfully built man in his early twenties, and wears swimming trunks and a striped beach hat. Carries a beach bag and a bottle of wine.)

IAN: *(Calls)* Ice cream, lolly ices, Durex!

JILL: You're just in time.

IAN: For what?

JILL: To oil me.

IAN: Aye aye! *(Sits on JILL's mattress.)* Shove up then.

JILL: Mind the wine!

IAN: You know, you've got a lovely bottom.

JILL: Oh, you've noticed?

IAN: Only it takes up half of the mattress.

JILL: I'm sorry ...

IAN: Where's the oil then?

JILL: Here.

(JILL gives him a bottle of oil from her bag and lies on her stomach. IAN oils her back and legs - making it evident that he enjoys feeling her, occasionally pushing his hand to her breasts and crotch, while she twists away and squirms, laughing, and he groans with exaggerated delight. EUNICE looks away, embarrassed.)

IAN: With you in a jiffy.

EUNICE: What?

IAN: You're next.

EUNICE: Oh!

JILL: I said oil me, not massage me.

IAN: It's got to be well rubbed in.

JILL: It's awfully kind of you.

IAN: Forget it.

(SANDY comes back and towels herself.)

(To SANDY) Hello darling!

SANDY: There was a big brown frog in the pool!

JILL: Probably an Arab prince.

SANDY: What? Some hope!

(ANDREW comes back, dries himself.)

EUNICE: Are you going into town?

ANDREW: If you feel like.

EUNICE: I'll stay here and have a read.

ANDREW: Oh ...

SANDY: Your husband's a great swimmer, isn't he?

EUNICE: Yes.

SANDY: He's been teaching me the butterfly.

IAN: Bully for you!

(EUNICE gets up.)

EUNICE: I'd better tell Ahmed we're not going on the tour.

ANDREW: You don't mind, do you?

EUNICE: No, we'll go next time. You take Sandy into town.

ANDREW: Are you sure you won't come?

EUNICE: No ... actually I want to finish my book.

(EUNICE goes off.)

IAN: Have you recovered?

JILL: Recovered?

IAN: From last night?

JILL: I'm recovering now.

SANDY: What happened last night?

IAN: Oh, you missed a great night at the disco.

SANDY: Oh?

IAN: Went on till about four o'clock.

ANDREW: I could hear it.

IAN: Did we keep you awake?

ANDREW: No ... no, we were reading. It was too hot to sleep.

SANDY: Who was there?

IAN: A big gang ... the Australians, and the Swedish couple, and the American crowd -

JILL: One of the American boys streaked through the bar.

SANDY: He streaked?

JILL: Yes. Ahmed almost jumped out of his sandals.

IAN: And what about the Irish girl?

JILL: Christ, yes! I must say I admire her stamina.

SANDY: Why?

IAN: She was in and out to her chalet every half hour with a different bloke.

JILL: *(Laughing)* Ian was shocked.

IAN: I was hell.

JILL: You were timing her.

IAN: She must have a cunt like Heathrow Airport.

JILL: Just because you weren't invited ...

IAN: I think she's getting a year's ration here.

JILL: All professional men, too.

IAN: Always the worst.

(MARTIN comes on, an athletic-looking man in his thirties, resplendent in a long kaftan and slippers, carrying a bottle of wine. He pulls down a mattress and sits.)

JILL: How are you?

MARTIN: What? Fine.

JILL: Andrew was telling me about your face.

MARTIN: Just a scratch.

JILL: Some 'scratch'!

MARTIN: Only needed a plaster.

JILL: *(Mimicking)* A plaaster!

MARTIN: I got a new one from the nurse.

JILL: How did you do it?

MARTIN: Tripped over a pepper tree.

(MARTIN looks at IAN as he applies the oil.)

She'll have you peeling oranges next.

IAN: Pleasure.

JILL: Have you had any breakfast?

MARTIN: Yes, I had two codeine and five black coffees.

(MARTIN sips a glass of wine, and grimaces.)

JILL: Go easy ...

MARTIN: What?

JILL: You'll have the runs again.

MARTIN: I've been running ever since I arrived here. I shall be carried home from this holiday on a stretcher. *(MARTIN lies back, stretches.)* God, I'm bushed. Last night ... that bloody hound ... the Alsatian or wolf or whatever it is ... came leaping out of the darkness at me, growling and barking ...

ANDREW: What did you do?

MARTIN: Showed him the cane and he slunk off.

JILL: Thank God they do have the dogs here.

MARTIN: Eh?

JILL: They've got to have them to keep out the Arabs.

MARTIN: They should teach them the difference between Arabs and Caucasians then. When you think ... right bloody holiday, this, with guard dogs and barbed-wire walls for protection. Worse than being with the regiment. Phew! What I'd give for a plate of bacon and eggs!

JILL: Oh, Martin!

MARTIN: What?

JILL: The food's not bad ... and Ahmed is laying on a

special lunch.

MARTIN: Special?

JILL: 'La haute cuisine Morocaine.'

MARTIN: What?

JILL: B'stila.

MARTIN: What's that?

JILL: Pigeon pie with cinnamon.

MARTIN: My God ...

JILL: You'll like it.

MARTIN: I'll never face Trafalgar Square again.

JILL: At least it'll be a change from all those greasy brochettes and that ghastly couscous. He can only do it because there'll only be a few of us here. Almost everybody is going on the tours.

MARTIN: Yes, I saw all the brats being loaded into the vans. Might have a bit of peace today.
(A BOY peers over the wall. He's an Arab of about sixteen. Ian notices him.)

BOY: Hi!

IAN: Bugger off!
(The BOY laughs and waves.)

BOY: Hello!

IAN: BUGGER OFF!
(IAN throws an orange at the BOY. It flies over the wall. The BOY vanishes.)

JILL: They're always hanging around here.

IAN: Pests.

SANDY: They're not doing any harm.

ANDREW: I wonder what they make of us?

IAN: Probably think we're all millionaires.

ANDREW: To them we are. In comparison to them the poorest person back home is rich.

MARTIN: Tell that to the unions.

IAN: Well, I gave him an orange, didn't I?

SANDY: Big deal!

(The BOY reappears on the wall. He laughs and waves.)

IAN: They are pests, aren't they?

BOY: Hi!

MARTIN: Salaam!

BOY: Have a good day!

JILL: I think he's been talking to the Yanks.

BOY: You happy?

(MARTIN goes near the wall.)

MARTIN: You speak English?

BOY: George Best!

MARTIN: *(To IAN)* I think he means you!

(The BOY makes a gesture of drinking. MARTIN holds up a bottle of Coke and the BOY nods eagerly.)

JILL: Martin —

MARTIN: What?

JILL: Don't encourage him.

MARTIN: I'm only giving him a drink.

(MARTIN slides open the bolts and opens the gates. There is a view of sandy grass and trees. The BOY stands cautiously a few feet away from the gates. He is bare-footed, wearing only trousers. MARTIN proffers the bottle.)

Here you are.

(The BOY steps forward to take it. JILL gets a camera.)

JILL: Martin —

MARTIN: What?

JILL: Can I get a photograph?

(MARTIN draws the BOY inside. He is a bit nervous and reluctant, but MARTIN gives him a bottle of Coke and gets him to stand holding up the bottle for the camera. JILL takes a couple of shots.)

MARTIN: Well done!

(MARTIN stands with his arms around the BOY's shoulder, posing. JILL takes the shot.)

JILL: Now you take me.

(JILL changes places with MARTIN.)

MARTIN: Say cheese.

JILL: *(Laughing)* Cheese cheese cheese.

(JILL tries to get the BOY to smile - grinning at him and tickling him, until he begins to giggle and laugh.)

MARTIN: Hold it!

(MARTIN takes a couple of shots.)

JILL: Thanks.

(JILL leaves the BOY. Picks up an orange and tosses it to him. He leaps after it. JILL tosses another orange and he scrambles after that. MARTIN takes more shots.

IAN picks up a bowl of sweets.)

IAN: Hey! Catch!

(IAN tosses a sweet high in the air. The BOY leaps for it.

JILL tosses another sweet. The BOY runs to get it.

MARTIN clicks the camera. The BOY holds his hands out, begging for more.

IAN points to his mouth, indicating that he wants the BOY to catch the sweets in his mouth.)

Get this, Martin!

(IAN tosses the sweets up, and the BOY jumps for them, his teeth snapping.)

Here boy! Here boy! Here!

(MARTIN takes shots while both IAN and JILL 'feed' the BOY.

Finally IAN throws the whole bowl of sweets in the air, and the BOY scrambles around collecting them.

ANDREW suddenly jumps up.)

ANDREW: Get out. Get out!

(ANDREW urges the BOY toward the gates. He retreats uncertainly.)

Go on ... out of here!

(ANDREW pulls some coins from his pockets, gives them to the BOY. Shoos him out and pushes the gates to. Comes back.)

You can't treat them like performing animals!

JILL: Don't be so damned pious.

MARTIN: Only a bit of fun.

ANDREW: Fun!

MARTIN: He enjoyed it as much as we did. Poor little bugger.

IAN: Have you seen them in the bins outside the camp, scavenging?

MARTIN: Yes, they collect empty jars and bottles and sell them in the Medina.

ANDREW: But doesn't it make you feel guilty?

MARTIN: What?

ANDREW: The idea of those boys scavenging for our leavings in the bins.

MARTIN: If it wasn't for us there wouldn't be anything in the bins.

ANDREW: They must hate us.

MARTIN: I don't agree.

ANDREW: What?

MARTIN: I think they envy us. They look at us and they probably think we spend all our lives like this ... No work and no responsibilities.

JILL: That's the way they spend *their* lives.

IAN: I wonder who's better off?

ANDREW: Would you swop?

JILL: Christ, let's forget it - There's bugger all we can do about it.

(Silence)

IAN: *(To MARTIN)* Is there much to do in the town?

MARTIN: No, but it's quite pleasant to sit in the square in the sunshine, sipping mint tea and watching the cripples.

IAN: The cripples?

MARTIN: Yes, there's a constant parade of the legless, the armless and the eyeless.

IAN: Jesus ...

ANDREW: And they're also workless and penniless ...

MARTIN: The amazing thing is they're so resilient. They sit there for hours sipping their revolting sweet drinks and chattering away quite cheerfully.

IAN: Can you understand them?

MARTIN: Yes, they speak French, of course. Funny, listening to them ... it's just like being back in London, in the club.

IAN: Is it?

MARTIN: Yes, they talk about the same sort of things, you know ... who's fucking who and how and when and who's not fucking who ... just like home.

(Pause)

I asked one man what they did when they were out in the desert. And he said, 'Well, there's always a man or a goat or a donkey ... and in the last resort you can always spit on your hands and do it yourself.'

IAN: *(Mock shock)* Dirty buggers!

MARTIN: Natural enough. I remember once, on an exercise in Germany, I caught one of my own men, a private soldier, jerking off into half a pound of lamb's liver.

ANDREW: Thank God it wasn't an officer!

JILL: And other barrack room ballads ...

MARTIN: I must say, though, they do seem to have quite an appetite over here.

JILL: No wonder they need four wives.

MARTIN: Fucking masochists.

JILL: Heavy, Martin, heavy!

ANDREW: Yes ... polygyny ...

MARTIN: Polygyny, polyandry ... polycock or polycunt ... Who cares as long as it works?

JILL: The women.

MARTIN: What?

JILL: How does it work for the women?

MARTIN: It's all changing ...

JILL: They're drifting toward monogamy while we're drifting toward polygamy.

MARTIN: Ahhh ... Islam!

ANDREW: Personally I'd trade the whole culture of Islam for a few factories and irrigation schemes. I mean ... you can't keep them suspended in this state indefinitely as a tourist attraction.

IAN: I thought the Arab states were all filthy rich ... groaning with oil money?

MARTIN: They're not rich in oil here, but they are rich in phosphate ... almost as valuable. And yet the poverty ... here, and throughout Arabia ...

IAN: Where's all the money going?

JILL: They're buying up Battersea.

MARTIN: If they're buying, we're selling.

IAN: Do you think they'll ever catch up?

MARTIN: With what?

IAN: With us.

MARTIN: God forbid. *(Pause)* Though I can tell you what the sheiks *are* doing ...

IAN: What?

MARTIN: They're clubbing together to build a huge mosque in Rome ... nine million pounds worth ...

IAN: In Rome?

MARTIN: Yes, next door to the Vatican.

IAN: But there can't be that many Moslems in Rome?

MARTIN: They're sending missionaries over, to convert us all.

ANDREW: Religion ... the sheik's best friend!

MARTIN: Hmmm ... Christianity is finished anyway, but it's had a good run for its money.

ANDREW: A good run for our money.

MARTIN: *(To SANDY)* What do you say?

(SANDY stares in surprise.)

Don't you ever say anything?

JILL: When she's got something worth saying.

MARTIN: If we all did that we'd never open our mouths. Well, my darling, I shall await your maiden speech with great interest.

(JILL gets up, taps SANDY.)

JILL: Let's go and have a dip.

(JILL and SANDY go off to the pool.)

MARTIN: Can't stand people being mysterious.

IAN: She's just shy.

MARTIN: Is that it? You probably know her better than I do.

IAN: Not really ...

ANDREW: She's on her own, isn't she?

IAN: Yes.

ANDREW: Surprising ...

IAN: Why?

ANDREW: Oh, a young girl like her ...

IAN: Young girls like her travel the world now with

a rucksack.

ANDREW: I know, but ... she's very pretty, isn't she?

MARTIN: If you like that sort of thing. I'm more surprised to find you on your own.

IAN: Me?

MARTIN: Yes.

IAN: Why?

MARTIN: Oh, young man like you, soccer star and all that ... shouldn't think you'd go short of crumpet?

IAN: Too much.

MARTIN: Too much?

IAN: It's got so when I think of women I think of fish.

MARTIN: Fish?

(IAN laughs, wrinkles his nose, sniffing.)

Are you very fit?

IAN: I won't be after a couple of weeks of this.

MARTIN: Take you on with the rope.

IAN: Right, Major ...

(MARTIN spreads a towel. Picks up a skipping rope and ties the ends together. He kneels at one end of the towel, Ian at the other, and they loop the rope around their necks. Start a tug of war with the neck. JILL comes on.)

JILL: Oh, not those games again!

(Finally MARTIN forces IAN down. MARTIN laughs. IAN slips the rope off and rubs his neck. Sits back.)

IAN: *(Rueful)* Jesus ...

MARTIN: Andrew?

ANDREW: I'm afraid I'm past it.

MARTIN: *(Delighted)* What, at your age? How about the bottle game?

JILL: Martin, lay off!

MARTIN: Livens things up a bit.

ANDREW: *(To IAN)* I used to play with a local team every
    weekend ... till I was in my thirties. Centre half.
    Then one afternoon a centre-forward put five past me
    and I realized I was middle-aged.

IAN: I won't be sorry when I am.

ANDREW: Why?

IAN: Find something interesting to do.

ANDREW: You don't enjoy playing?

IAN: Football's all right, but it's the fans ... you
    want to stand on the pitch and hear twenty thousand
    of them screaming from the terraces. Fucking maniacs!
    Makes me go cold. Talk about the Roman arena! No,
    once I pack it in, you won't catch me near a football
    match.

ANDREW: Not even to watch?

IAN: Too dangerous.

ANDREW: Yes ... but the basic reason for -

MARTIN: 'Far are the shades of Arabia,
    Where the princes ride at noon ...'
    *(MARTIN stands, stretches, looks around. Drinks his
    wine and spits it out.)*
    I can't drink this piss. Let's have a proper drink ...

IAN: I'll get them. What'll you have?

MARTIN: Oh ... I'll have a Scotch.

JILL: Campari, please.

IAN: Andrew?

ANDREW: I'll stick to the old Chaudsoleil, thanks.
    (IAN goes off for the drinks.)

JILL: Martin, you are a swine.

MARTIN: Ian's a nice boy, isn't he?

JILL: You've scared the life out of that poor girl.

MARTIN: Rubbish!

JILL: She won't come out of the pool.

ANDREW: I'll go over ...

(ANDREW goes off to the pool.)

MARTIN: This place is full of nice chaps.

JILL: Fuck you.

MARTIN: Easy, old girl.

JILL: Why do you always have to fuck things up? Why did you turn on her?

MARTIN: Who?

JILL: Sandy.

MARTIN: Thought she looked left out of the fun.

JILL: That's gallant! And what about Andrew? Why are you always needling him?

MARTIN: Oh, he gets on my tit.

JILL: Why?

MARTIN: There's something about him. I dunno ... He's like a monk gone wrong.

JILL: God ... and you're not even pissed yet ...

MARTIN: I'm pacing myself.

JILL: I thought you were going to dry out. *(JILL touches MARTIN's cheek to look at the cut.)* Is that all right?

MARTIN: Don't fuss.

JILL: You're not going over there again today, are you?

MARTIN: Why not?

JILL: You're taking a risk ...

MARTIN: Rubbish.

JILL: No wonder you were so determined to come here. I'm beginning to think we ought to take our holidays separately.

MARTIN: Then we'd *never* see each other.

JILL: No.

MARTIN: Is that what you want?

JILL: I don't know ...

MARTIN: Are you worried about me ... or about our fellow

campers?

JILL: I don't give a fuck about our fellow campers. How do you think I feel about you after you've been with ... with them.

MARTIN: Who?

JILL: Those Arab boys ...

MARTIN: Would you prefer me to try Arab girls?

JILL: Or goats or donkeys ... I don't care what you do on this holiday. If you want to go into town and get sliced, that's your affair. I don't care if you are found in the Medina with a knife in your back and your prick stuffed in your mouth.

MARTIN: I've never had it stuffed in there before.

JILL: But don't fuck everyone else up!

MARTIN: Whatever you say, dear. You know that all that matters to me is your happiness.

JILL: I'll look after that.

(MARTIN kisses her on the cheek.)

You don't do that very often.

MARTIN: Don't want to cheapen the gesture. I thought you were enjoying yourself.

JILL: I'm revelling in it.

MARTIN: Jill ...

JILL: What?

MARTIN: Let's just try ...

JILL: Try what?

MARTIN: Let's just try and enjoy ourselves on this holiday.

JILL: Will you try?

MARTIN: Yes.

JILL: Will you go easy on the booze?

MARTIN: Why, is it running short?

(JILL laughs.)

JILL: Come to the disco tonight.

MARTIN: The disco?

JILL: Yes ... you'd like it.

MARTIN: Hardly my style ...

JILL: Please. We could have a drink and a chat ...

MARTIN: You can't chat with that din.

JILL: We could ask Ahmed to serve dinner out here. There'll only be a few of us. It'd be fun out here ...

MARTIN: What ... with Karl Marx over there agonizing about the plight of the Arabs ...

JILL: I know he's a bit of a bore. All these second-hand agonies. But you do provoke him and you know he's got no sense of humour -

MARTIN: Rubbish.

JILL: You know you do.

MARTIN: Livens things up.

JILL: Like hammering nails ...

(IAN returns with the drinks.)

IAN: Oh, that smell ...

JILL: Mmmm.

MARTIN: It's pigeon pie.

JILL: And cinnamon.

IAN: It's mint, isn't it?

JILL: Yes ... my favourite smell.

IAN: You get plenty of it here.

JILL: What's your favourite smell?

IAN: It's one I couldn't mention in mixed company.

JILL: Oh, really?

(IAN passes round the drinks.

SANDY comes back from the pool and goes to the draughts set. After a moment she is joined by ANDREW.)

MARTIN: Cheers!

IAN: Cheers.

IAN: *(To JILL)* Your turn.

JILL: What?

IAN: The oil ...

JILL: Pleasure. *(JILL oils IAN)* You need it.

IAN: Easy ... I'm sore.

JILL: You're going all pink.

IAN: That's why I came here.

JILL: Last year I had to do a campaign about the English beach resorts. You know ... Torquay, Scarborough, Morecambe, all those seaside middens.

IAN: 'Middens'?

JILL: Yes ... drizzling promenades and nymphets puking in the sand and steamy cafés serving curried prawns with chips and jingling amusement arcades ...

IAN: You must have written a great campaign.

JILL: It was imaginative. My idea of hell would be to be locked forever in an amusement arcade.

IAN: With no coins.

JILL: With coins. *(JILL finishes the oiling and rubs her hands together)* Christ that's sticky.

IAN: It's my sweat.

JILL: Ugghh.

(JILL lies back. IAN relaxes and sips his drink.)

IAN: Ahh ... lovely.

MARTIN: Nice to have a proper drink.

IAN: I thought this was a dry country?

JILL: With Martin around no country's dry. 'Your guide to Alcoholidays.'

MARTIN: For a dry country they import a hell of a lot of Scotch whisky. Allah is no match for alcohol. It's ruining the religion, like sex in England.

JILL: Religion has ruined sex for long enough.

IAN: Oh? I hadn't noticed.

(JILL stretches)

JILL: Oh boy! Feel that sun!

MARTIN: *(Sings)*

'When it's springtime in Morocco,
I'll be coming back to you,
When it's springtime in Morocco,
And your lovely eyes are blue,

Once again I'll say I love you,
Where the birds sing all the day,
When it's springtime in Morocco,
In Morocco far away.'

IAN: 'Let's Maroc around the clock tonight ...'

MARTIN: That's damned good!

(EUNICE returns, sits.)

ANDREW: Did you see Ahmed?

EUNICE: Yes.

ANDREW: Have they gone?

EUNICE: Who?

ANDREW: The tours.

EUNICE: Yes. The place is deserted.

(EUNICE glances at a paperback.

ANDREW and SANDY play draughts.

MARTIN takes some postcards from the beach bag and looks at them.)

MARTIN: What the hell can you put on a postcard? It's too small and yet it's too big.

JILL: I'll do them.

MARTIN: I wonder what Lawrence of Arabia put on his postcards?

(MARTIN begins scribbling. Stops.)

'Still eyes look coldly upon him,
Cold voices whisper and say,
He is crazed with the spell of far Arabia,
They have stolen his wits away.'

JILL: I know what's stolen your wits away.

MARTIN: Used to love that sort of poetry. You know,

Masefield, Chesterton, Walter de la Mare. Not like
this po-faced drivel you read today. Not that I do
read it. Can't understand a word of it. Bloody
rubbish.

(MARTIN resumes scribbling.

JILL lies on her stomach and unfastens her bikini
straps to tan her back.

The muezzin calls from the minaret. All listen.

EUNICE listens intently.

ANDREW looks at her, smiles, touches her shoulder.)

ANDREW: All right?

EUNICE: That call ...

ANDREW: What?

EUNICE: Nothing.

SANDY: It's only the muezzin summoning the faithful.

EUNICE: I know what it is.

SANDY: *(Reads from the primer)*

> 'Allah is greatest,
> I testify that there is no God save Allah
> and that Muhammad is the apostle of Allah,
> Up to prayer, up to salvation,
> Allah is greatest,
> There is no god save Allah.'

EUNICE: It woke me this morning.

SANDY: They do it five times a day. They turn toward
Mecca and pray.

JILL: Five times a day, down tools and pray. It's worse
than having jets flying over.

EUNICE: Do you get the feeling ...

ANDREW: What?

EUNICE: Well ... that you shouldn't be listening?

IAN: It's only a tape recording.

MARTIN: *(To EUNICE)* Are you religious?

EUNICE: I don't go to church.

MARTIN: No, I mean ... d'you believe in ...

EUNICE: I believe. I still have my faith. I couldn't offer any rational arguments but I believe in my bones.

MARTIN: Huh ... I believe in my bones too. Bones, booze and balls, I believe in.

JILL: Martin ...

MARTIN: What?

JILL: Have you finished with those cards?

MARTIN: At least these people live their religion.

ANDREW: That's because it's all they've got ... like football pools in England.

MARTIN: At least they take it seriously. Not like the Church in the West ... glorified registry office and funeral parlour.

ANDREW: Yes, but when you look at them ... diseased, illiterate, and scrabbling for food ...

MARTIN: They help each other.

ANDREW: What?

MARTIN: Charity.

ANDREW: A device for maintaining the social hierarchy.

MARTIN: Rubbish.

ANDREW: They don't need Allah. What these people need is a revolution, not a revelation.

JILL: Have you finished the cards?

MARTIN: What?

JILL: The cards.

MARTIN: Oh yes.

JILL: I'll sign them.

(JILL takes the cards and sits up, clutching the bikini straps. Looks at the cards and laughs.)

Oh God ... you're not serious?

MARTIN: What?

JILL: Where on earth did you get these?

MARTIN: In the town.

JILL: They're dreadful.

MARTIN: Give 'em a giggle back home.

JILL: *(To IAN)* Just look at these.

(JILL passes the cards to IAN.)

IAN: *(Laughs)* Looks like Omar Sharif on top of Britt Ekland.

JILL: Couldn't you get any others?

MARTIN: They're all like that. The Arabs love 'em.

JILL: *(Reads)* 'I'd be happy to die here.' Isn't that rather a morbid message?

MARTIN: I'm not one of those geniuses who can dash off a postcard. Just put your X on them.

(JILL signs the cards and slips them into the bag. As she does so she struggles to hold the bikini top, which slips.)

JILL: Ooops ...

(JILL clutches the bikini.)

MARTIN: Why don't you either tie that thing up or take it off?

JILL: That's an idea ...

(JILL looks at MARTIN. Takes off the bikini top and lies back.

MARTIN grins. The others look on.)

IAN: Bra-vo!

JILL: Ha. *(JILL looks at herself)* Oh, they look obscene ...

MARTIN: What?

JILL: White boobs.

MARTIN: They are rather prominent.

JILL: The only time I've ever had a real tan was in Yugoslavia. I had a real all-over tan. It was marvellous. All over.

(MARTIN looks at JILL, smiles.)

MARTIN: Well ...

(JILL takes off the bikini pants and lies back.)
Ian?

*(IAN grins, hesitates, takes off his trunks.
MARTIN takes off his kaftan, then glances around - he
is enjoying stage-managing this.)*
Andrew?

*(ANDREW stands self-consciously looking at, and away
from, the others.)*

ANDREW: What about you?

MARTIN: Oh, after you ...

*(ANDREW seems paralysed.
Suddenly SANDY strips and lies back on the mattress.)*

EUNICE: Oh, my God ...

JILL: Come on, Eunice ...

EUNICE: What?

JILL: Enjoy the sunshine.

EUNICE: I am, thanks.

JILL: Andrew, you must be used to nudity.

ANDREW: In the surgery, yes.

JILL: *(To EUNICE)* You look as if you want to make some kind of statement.

EUNICE: I think you're making the statement.

JILL: Well, I wish you wouldn't stand there like a nun in a brothel, you're making me embarrassed.

EUNICE: I'm sorry.

ANDREW: Eunice ...

EUNICE: I know it's terribly unsophisticated of me, but I do find the sight of bare bodies boring.

JILL: Boring?

EUNICE: Yes.

JILL: You must see too many.

MARTIN: Actually I think it's rather refreshing.

EUNICE: You would.

ANDREW: Eunice —

EUNICE: What?

ANDREW: Be reasonable ...

EUNICE: Are you going to strip?

ANDREW: Oh hell ...

JILL: Why don't you two fuck off and discuss it in your chalet?

EUNICE: Why don't you go off and sunbathe somewhere private?

(Pause. ANDREW sits down.)

ANDREW: Let's just enjoy the sunshine.

MARTIN: Damned good idea.

IAN: Feel that sun!

SANDY: Super!

JILL: Ahhh ... freedom!

(EUNICE begins unbuttoning her blouse.

ANDREW stares at her.)

ANDREW: Eunice.

(EUNICE begins peeling off the blouse.)

Eunice!

EUNICE: What?

ANDREW: Don't be ridiculous.

EUNICE: Ridiculous? Me ridiculous?

JILL: Oh, for Christ's sake!

(ANDREW takes EUNICE's arm.)

ANDREW: Let's go back to the chalet.

EUNICE: No.

ANDREW: Oh, come on ...

EUNICE: No.

(EUNICE frees her arm.)

ANDREW: Eunice ... Act your age.

EUNICE: My age? Is that what's wrong?

(EUNICE goes off.)

JILL: I suddenly feel like a swim.

(JILL puts on her bikini and goes off to the pool. IAN slips on his trunks and follows her.)

MARTIN: Phew! Things have livened up a bit!

(MARTIN turns to SANDY, who wraps herself in a white bath towel.)

Where did that all come from?

ANDREW: I'm sorry ...

MARTIN: Have a drink.

ANDREW: No thanks. Eunice has been tense ever since we arrived here. I mean ... she *is* at that age ... you know ... and ...

MARTIN: It's the heat.

ANDREW: It's the whole thing. I mean, she was shocked, really shocked, by the town yesterday. We've never been outside Europe before and I think she expected something like, well, southern Spain. It's not easy to relax and enjoy yourself when you know people are suffering like that.

SANDY: That's what's so unreal ...

ANDREW: What?

SANDY: While they're suffering we're arguing about ... sex, and personal problems.

MARTIN: When they stop suffering they'll start arguing about sex, and personal problems. Like a drink?

(SANDY ignores him.)

ANDREW: No thanks.

MARTIN: Young lady ... Sorry if I seemed rather offhand earlier on. Just wanted to get a response from you, see what you were thinking ...

SANDY: I think you're a pain in the arse.

MARTIN: You know ... you're absolutely right.

> *(MARTIN goes off for a drink.*
>
> *SANDY huddles in the bath towel.*
>
> *ANDREW looks at her, turns to go off, hesitates, turns back.)*

ANDREW: I hope we haven't put you off going into the town.

SANDY: No.

ANDREW: You still want to go?

SANDY: I want to see what it's like for myself.

ANDREW: You might even like it.

SANDY: I've been forewarned.

ANDREW: No, I mean ... you're different.

SANDY: 'Different'?

ANDREW: Eunice is too sensitive in some ways, I mean, she's been sheltered for too long. She hasn't really seen anything of the world. What can you see from a semi in the suburbs?

SANDY: I suppose it must come as a shock.

ANDREW: Yes. But she'll be all right. I'm glad you're here.

ANDREW: Oh ... ?

ANDREW: I can't say I find this crowd exactly ... my type.

SANDY: They're not too bad ...

ANDREW: But the way they behaved with that boy!

SANDY: Yes.

ANDREW: The master race! My God ...

SANDY: I think they're fairly typical.

ANDREW: You aren't.

SANDY: I think I should have gone with my boy friend.

ANDREW: Where's he gone?

SANDY: The Canaries.

ANDREW: Didn't they appeal to you?

SANDY: They're over-run.

> *(Pause)*

43

ANDREW: Do you live with him?

SANDY: No ... I would do, but he's only got a three-foot bed.

ANDREW: Three foot long?

SANDY: What do you take him for ... a midget? Three foot wide!

ANDREW: I must say ... meeting you has made this holiday for me.

SANDY: Huh ...

ANDREW: Otherwise it would have been a dead loss.

SANDY: Well ... I'm glad.

(SANDY smiles at ANDREW. Pause.)

ANDREW: Why don't we go over into the town now?

SANDY: Now?

ANDREW: I don't fancy hanging round here.

SANDY: All right.

ANDREW: I'll just go and see Eunice. See you in a few minutes.

(ANDREW goes off. SANDY watches him go. Then she gets up, wrapping the towel around her. Picks up a bottle of wine and drinks from it. Picks up the primer. Glances at it. Goes to the gates and looks outside. Calls.)

SANDY: Hi!

(The BOY appears near the gates.)

Ente walad Keslan!

(SANDY reads this from the primer, meaning 'You are an idle boy'. The BOY looks uncomprehending. SANDY sips wine from the bottle. The BOY makes the gesture of drinking. SANDY gives him the bottle and he swigs. SANDY and the BOY pass away from the gateway, and out of sight.

After a moment JILL and IAN come on from the pool.

They dry themselves.)

JILL: That woman ...

IAN: Pathetic.

JILL: Sanctimonious cow!

IAN: She said she found it boring but she looked to me as if she was going to throw a fit.

JILL: 'Boring'! The prude's cop-out!

IAN: Do you fancy going to the beach?

JILL: The beach?

IAN: Yes ... 'Miles and miles of lonely sand, lined with mimosa ...'

JILL: You've been reading the brochure.

IAN: So have you.

JILL: Is it far?

IAN: No ... ten minutes' walk.

JILL: Why do you want to go to the beach?

IAN: To fuck.

(JILL raises her sunglasses.)

JILL: Why has it taken you three days to ask me?

IAN: I was waiting for you to ask me.

JILL: Oh, you are liberated, aren't you?

IAN: Will you?

JILL: When do you want to go?

IAN: Now. Before *they* come back.

JILL: All right.

IAN: You will?

JILL: Why not?

IAN: What about Martin?

JILL: You want to ask him too? Here he is ...

(MARTIN returns with a drink.)

MARTIN: Don't blame me.

JILL: What?

MARTIN: Holiday's running true to form.

IAN: How do you mean?

MARTIN: Almost every holiday I've been on has ended in blows.

IAN: Have they?

MARTIN: You hear about holiday romances but I think there are far more holiday divorces.

(Pause)

JILL: We were thinking of going to the beach.

MARTIN: Who?

JILL: Ian and I.

MARTIN: Oh?

JILL: D'you fancy it?

MARTIN: You're not asking the others?

JILL: Huh!

MARTIN: No ...

JILL: D'you fancy going?

MARTIN: Oh, I don't know ...

JILL: I don't fancy staying here.

MARTIN: No.

JILL: We could have some fun at the beach.

MARTIN: The three of us?

JILL: Yes ...

(MARTIN smiles.)

MARTIN: The only trouble with the beach is the bloody sand.

JILL: We'll take towels.

MARTIN: And there's the flies ...

JILL: Come with us.

MARTIN: When do you want to go?

JILL: Now.

MARTIN: Hang on –

JILL: What?

MARTIN: We'll miss the pigeon pie.

JILL: I'm sure Ahmed will save you some.

MARTIN: I dunno ...

JILL: Come with us. You'll enjoy it.

(Pause)

MARTIN: I think I might just get my head down for a while.

(JILL collects her things, as does IAN.)

JILL: Suit yourself.

(JILL and IAN go off.

MARTIN is left alone for a moment. He drains his drink. ANDREW comes on, glances at MARTIN, goes off to the pool. Comes back. Puts on shirt and trousers.)

ANDREW: D'you know where Sandy is?

(MARTIN shakes his head. Begins collecting his things. Puts on his kaftan.)

We're going into town.

MARTIN: She was gone when I came back from the bar.

ANDREW: Oh ... I wonder where she's got to?

MARTIN: She's probably in her chalet.

ANDREW: No.

MARTIN: She's probably in somebody else's chalet then.

ANDREW: There's nobody else here. And anyway, if she'd gone back to the chalets I would have seen her passing.

MARTIN: Oh, she'll turn up. Young girl like her ... never know what she'll get up to. She's at that age, you know ... head in the clouds. *(Gathers his things)* Up to prayer, up to salvation!

(MARTIN goes off.

ANDREW looks around, puzzled. Then he goes to the gates and steps outside, glances left and right. EUNICE comes on.)

EUNICE: *(Calls)* Andrew.

(ANDREW comes back on.)

47

I think I would like to go into the town after all.
ANDREW: Oh.
EUNICE: You don't mind do you?
ANDREW: I asked you to come.
EUNICE: Yes ... I know, but ... *(Pause)* I'm sorry about all that ... before.
ANDREW: Oh, that's all right.
EUNICE: Forgive me? I've been feeling a bit on edge. I don't know if it's the heat, or the food, or ... anyway, I am sorry.
ANDREW: Doesn't matter.
EUNICE: I should have either just ignored them when they stripped ... or gone off and left them to it. Forgive me?
ANDREW: I'm worried about Sandy.
EUNICE: You're worried.
ANDREW: She's just vanished. I mean, she didn't go back to the chalet, but she's not in the pool, and she's not in the bar ...
EUNICE: Maybe she's gone out?
ANDREW: What, for a stroll in the woods?
EUNICE: I wouldn't put it past her.
ANDREW: Without her things? *(ANDREW indicates SANDY's mattress. He kneels down by it. Picks up the bikini top.)* I can't understand it. I said I'd see her back here.
EUNICE: Do you enjoy fingering that?

(ANDREW puts the bikini down.)

ANDREW: I think I'd better have a word with Ahmed.
EUNICE: Ahmed?
ANDREW: Yes.
EUNICE: But why?
ANDREW: Well, it is a bit alarming, isn't it? I left her

here and when I came back the gates were open and
she'd gone.

EUNICE: But you can't go running round after her.

(ANDREW goes back to the gates, steps outside, walks off.

EUNICE looks round, now alarmed.

After a moment ANDREW returns.)

ANDREW: Look at this.

EUNICE: What is it?

ANDREW: Sandy's book.

EUNICE: Where was it?

ANDREW: It was lying on the ground there ... a few yards along. On the grass.

EUNICE: So she must have gone out ...

ANDREW: But she wouldn't go without her things ... and then the book ...

(ANDREW starts off.)

EUNICE: Where are you going?

ANDREW: To get Ahmed.

EUNICE: But what can he do?

ANDREW: He can get the dogs.

(ANDREW goes off.)

EUNICE: *(Shocked)* The dogs?

(EUNICE hurries off after ANDREW.)

BLACKOUT

Scene 2

Early afternoon.
JILL comes on, wearing her kaftan, followed by IAN in jeans and sweatshirt. JILL takes off the kaftan, under which she wears her bikini.

IAN: Fancy that pigeon pie?
JILL: Too late.
IAN: I could ask Ahmed ...
JILL: I'm not hungry. You go ...
IAN: No, I'm not hungry.
JILL: Where is everyone? *(JILL sits, puts some oil on.)* Christ, you've ruined my bikini.
IAN: I'm sorry ...
JILL: You're a menace to womanhood. Are you always like tha
IAN: I can't help it.
JILL: You might have warned me.
IAN: I'm sorry.
JILL: What a flop!
IAN: If you hadn't touched me ...
JILL: Ha! If I hadn't touched you ... What did you expect after that build-up? After all that licking and biting and kissing and rolling around the sandhill. I was *aching*. So I touch you ... and WHAM BAM THANK YOU MAM!
IAN: I couldn't help it.
JILL: So I'm left gasping ... and all you can do is lie there like a wet sock. I could have more fun with my thumb. *(JILL gets a drink.)* Christ ... red hot wine! *(Sips)* Have you thought about seeing a doctor?
IAN: I did.

JILL: What did he say?

IAN: He said I was suffering from a hair-trigger.

JILL: You're not suffering from it, I am.

IAN: He said it's quite common.

JILL: Isn't there anything they can do?

IAN: He suggested that I try and think about something else at the critical moment.

JILL: Like what?

IAN: Oh anything ... Politics.

JILL: The passion killer?

IAN: Yes.

(JILL laughs)

JILL: Have you tried?

IAN: It doesn't work for me.

JILL: No.

IAN: I did try some pills that slow you down ... help you to defer it ... but you can't keep using them or they lead to impotence.

JILL: That might be the best solution.

(Sound of dogs barking. JILL rubs her crotch.)

Now for my pleasures I'm burning again.

IAN: I'm sorry.

JILL: It's not your fault, it's cystitis.

IAN: What?

JILL: Itchy cunt.

IAN: Oh ...

JILL: Bacterial, not sexual. I'd just got over an infection. Christ, when you think ... as if periods and pregnancy weren't enough, a woman has to put up with cystitis and thrush and pleurisy and vaginitis ... all the little maladies of the cunt. What does a man have to put up with?

IAN: Women.

(EUNICE comes on.)

EUNICE: Oh, you're back ...

JILL: Where is everyone?

EUNICE: Have you seen anything of Sandy?

JILL: No. Not since this morning. Why?

EUNICE: She's missing.

JILL: Missing?

EUNICE: Yes ... she's nowhere around.

JILL: What do you mean, 'missing'?

EUNICE: We'd arranged to go into town with her but she's just vanished. She's not in her chalet, or -

JILL: Maybe she went ahead on her own?

EUNICE: No, she hasn't gone out. We asked the man on the main gate.

JILL: That old Arab?

EUNICE: Yes.

JILL: I wouldn't trust him.

EUNICE: Why?

JILL: He's full of hash.

EUNICE: He'd still have seen her if she'd gone out.

IAN: Have you looked in the disco?

EUNICE: Oh, of course ... we've looked everywhere. She's just not in here. But her things are still here ...

(JILL looks at the mattress.)

JILL: Maybe she went back to her chalet and got changed.

EUNICE: No ... we'd have seen her. *(Pause)* Andrew found her book outside ... you know that Arab primer she was reading from ...

JILL: Outside?

EUNICE: Yes ... outside the gates, a few yards away, on the grass. The gates were open.

IAN: Yes ... Martin opened them this morning.

JILL: Where is Martin?

EUNICE: I don't know.

JILL: Is he missing too?

EUNICE: The only reason we're worried about Sandy is because of her things ... and the book lying outside ...

JILL: Are you suggesting a gang of Arabs might have burst in and carried her off?

EUNICE: I'm not suggesting anything.

JILL: I don't think they'd have the nerve. The ones I've seen are such pathetic specimens.

EUNICE: I don't trust them ...

JILL: But I must admit I wouldn't go roaming around on my own here.

EUNICE: Do you think Sandy would?

JILL: She might.

(Sound of the dogs outside.)

EUNICE: Andrew's out there now, searching, with Ahmed.

JILL: Let's go and have a look.

IAN: I'll go.

JILL: What?

IAN: You'd better stay here.

JILL: Why?

IAN: In case she turns up.

(IAN goes out of the gates. JILL follows him. Looks outside then comes back in.)

JILL: What did Ahmed say?

EUNICE: He said the gates should be kept locked.

JILL: Now that's very helpful.

EUNICE: He said there are so many odd characters drifting around here, that ... well, it's not wise to go out on your own.

JILL: I can't really believe she'd have gone out. Though I don't know ... I wouldn't be surprised if she came dancing back in here with a bunch of flowers in her hand. That's the thing about girls of her age now ... They're not like us. I mean they expect to just throw their jeans on and go anywhere and do anything just like a man.

EUNICE: You might get away with that in Europe but not over here.

JILL: They're willing to take the risk.

EUNICE: Is this what you meant this morning ... when you called her a 'twentieth-century virgin'?

JILL: God knows what I meant this morning! *(Laughs)* But I suppose ... yes, I did mean that she had a kind of trusting quality that we lost when we were little girls.

EUNICE: 'Trusting'?

JILL: She trusts people - even men. She likes men ... she actually likes them. I don't think I've ever liked a man in my life ... I've admired men, or fancied men, or loved men, but I don't think I've ever just *liked* a man! And Sandy probably likes sex too. I've certainly never just liked sex. I've been too hung-up about it. But she isn't. She's not afraid of sex and neither is her generation. That's why they don't get used-up like us. Christ, for us sex means war, for them it means warmth. Sexual warmth! Can you imagine it? Compared with them, I'm still at the stage of buying love potions and weaving spells. I don't think I've ever been direct with a man in my life. Have you?

EUNICE: Do you think men want you to be direct?

JILL: I suppose it depends on their age. But how can you tell? There are as many radical pensioners as there are reactionary adolescents. 'Do you mind if I'm direct with you sir?' 'Not at all.' 'Then would you mind fucking me and fucking off?' *(Laughs)* No ... I'm an old-fashioned girl. I lie about my lust and I expect the man to lie about his feelings. At least the kids have cut out all that bullshit.

EUNICE: But is it all ...

JILL: I suppose you think I'm some kind of nympho?

EUNICE: No ...

JILL: I don't want to be too statistical about it, but I am thirty-eight and I've only fucked seven men.

EUNICE: You keep count?

JILL: I remember. Don't you?

EUNICE: That's not difficult.

JILL: What?

EUNICE: There's only been one ...

JILL: Really?

EUNICE: We were only seventeen when we got married.

JILL: Childhood sweethearts?

EUNICE: Yes.

JILL: Do you regret it?

EUNICE: No. But I don't think we'd marry each other if we met for the first time now.

JILL: Who would? Have you ever fancied anyone else?

EUNICE: No.

JILL: Oh boy!

EUNICE: What?

JILL: That must be some kind of record.

EUNICE: I don't think I'm unique.

JILL: You're certainly unconventional.

EUNICE: I'm always accused of being the opposite.

JILL: What about Andrew?

EUNICE: What?

JILL: Does he have other ... women?

EUNICE: I think that's the trouble.

55

JILL: What, he does?

EUNICE: No, he doesn't. I don't mean that he'd ever admit it, even to himself, but ... I'm dreading the next few years.

JILL: Why?

EUNICE: This is the first year we've ever had alone together. The children have gone.

JILL: You should be jumping for joy!

EUNICE: Why?

JILL: You'll probably find that you have more fun with Andrew than you've ever had.

EUNICE: That wouldn't be difficult.

JILL: Speaking for myself, I think the less parents and children see of each other, the more chance they have.

EUNICE: Who?

JILL: What?

EUNICE: The parents or the children?

JILL: Both, I should say.

EUNICE: It's ironic. For the last few years, I've been praying for them to go, and now that they're gone, I'm dreading it.

JILL: What made you think I didn't have any kids?

EUNICE: You haven't, have you?

JILL: No, but what made you think it?

EUNICE: You just struck me as a career woman.

JILL: Ouch!

EUNICE: I'm sorry ... but you do have a job, don't you?

JILL: I'm a copywriter. It's only a small company –

EUNICE: Don't apologize.

JILL: I wasn't. You don't have a job?

EUNICE: No, just the children ...

JILL: Don't apologize.

EUNICE: I was.

(They laugh.)

JILL: How many have you got?

EUNICE: Three. Maybe that was our mistake.

JILL: What?

EUNICE: Three were too many ... but then two were too few. *(Pause)* I envy you and Martin.

JILL: Huh! Why?

EUNICE: You seem very free.

JILL: So free I could puke sometimes.

EUNICE: Yes, but ... I wish I could be like that. I get so ... ridden, with jealousy ... I frighten myself. *(Pause)* Sometimes I think that Andrew only stays with me out of pity.

JILL: Oh, come on Eunice!

EUNICE: What?

JILL: He's not that fucking moral.

EUNICE: I think he is. Do you get jealous of Martin?

JILL: No.

EUNICE: But does he have other women?

JILL: No, he doesn't have other women. You know the way some men will chat you up and then ... hand on heart ... they say: 'There's something I must tell you ... I'm married.' Well, the first time I met Martin ... at a party ... he put a drink in my hand and said: 'There's something I must tell you ... I'm queer.' That was the word he used ... 'queer'.

EUNICE: So what happened?

JILL: I fell instantly in love with him. And I think he did with me. I thought I'd converted him. But I'd only converted him to me.

EUNICE: What?

JILL: There was a period when I would have been delighted to hear that he was screwing some other woman. But it

57

never happened.

EUNICE: I'd no idea ...

JILL: He doesn't carry a banner.

EUNICE: I'm sorry.

JILL: It's been a damned good match. He may be an old stoat but then I'm no angel. It's worked pretty well. Not that we see all that much of each other ...

EUNICE: Oh?

JILL: He's been posted all over the world.

EUNICE: And you stay in London?

JILL: Too right I do.

EUNICE: Where is he now?

JILL: Aldershot.

(JILL looks outside, comes back.)

I wonder what could have happened? The trouble is I hardly know her. I don't think we've exchanged more than a dozen words with each other. She keeps herself to herself ...

EUNICE: Not entirely.

JILL: What?

EUNICE: She often chats to Andrew.

JILL: And Ian ...

EUNICE: Yes ...

JILL: I suppose she finds that more fun than chatting with us old hags. I hope she's all right.

EUNICE: I wish we'd all gone on the tour.

JILL: Huh ... Yes, I do too.

EUNICE: Jill ...

JILL: What?

EUNICE: About this morning ...

JILL: Oh, forget it. Have a drink.

EUNICE: No thanks.

(JILL drinks.

Sound of dogs barking outside.

EUNICE and JILL look at each other, listening.)

JILL: Strange ... I wonder if she could have gone into town?

EUNICE: Have you been in?

JILL: Martin took me to the Government shop but I didn't really see the town.

EUNICE: It's quite an experience.

JILL: Is it?

EUNICE: Especially for a woman. God knows it was bad enough for me with Andrew, but if she has gone on her own ...

JILL: What?

EUNICE: We spent half an hour walking through the Medina and by the time I got out I was almost fainting. All those reeking carcasses covered in flies ... and that sweet smell, sweet sickly smell, like hash and mint, everywhere, everywhere you went. I could hardly breathe ... There were blind men feeling their way along with one hand and holding out begging cans with the other ... And the cripples ... so many cripples ... I saw a man on the ground with stumps for limbs ... scuttling through the crowd like a crab ... And the streets are so crowded ... not streets, more like alleyways, so narrow you have to go single file. I had to go behind Andrew, hanging on to his shirt. You're jammed into the crowd with no way out and all the time the men are staring at you and pressing against you. Their hands are all over you ... oh, not the Italian pinch on the bottom, I mean they're really feeling your body and squeezing and ... groping at you ...

JILL: Sounds just like the Tube.

EUNICE: No. No, it's not like the Tube.

(Sound of shouting outside.)

JILL: What's that?

EUNICE: Sounds like Andrew ...

(JILL goes to the gates and looks outside.)

What is it.

JILL: Oh my God.

(JILL steps outside. Sound of voices. EUNICE stares at the gates, not moving. ANDREW appears carrying *SANDY naked. JILL runs in past him.)*

ANDREW: A towel.

EUNICE: What ...?

ANDREW: Get a towel!

(JILL takes her bath towel and drapes it round SANDY.)

JILL: What happened?

ANDREW: Let's get her to the chalet.

EUNICE: What happened?

ANDREW: Get the nurse.

JILL: Is she all right?

ANDREW: She's been raped.

JILL: She's what?

EUNICE: Raped?

JILL: Oh my God!

(ANDREW starts off.

JILL looks at SANDY's face.)

ANDREW: Let's get her to the chalet.

JILL: Is she -

ANDREW: Get the nurse quick!

(IAN stands at the gate.

ANDREW goes off carrying SANDY followed by EUNICE.)

JILL: Raped?

IAN: Come on ...

JILL: Who by?

IAN: Arabs. Two Arabs.

JILL: *(With horror)* Two Arabs?

   (IAN takes JILL's arm.)

IAN: Come on, Jill.

JILL: What?

IAN: We'd better get Ahmed.

JILL: Ahmed?

IAN: He's around the other side.

   (JILL is frozen.)

JILL: That young girl ... raped?

IAN: Yeah ... come on.

JILL: Where's Martin?

IAN: What?

JILL: Martin ... where is he? *(A cry)* Where's Martin?

IAN: I don't know.

JILL: Oh God ...

   (JILL runs off. IAN goes back to the gates. Slams them shut.)

IAN: Animals. Fucking animals!

   BLACKOUT

ACT TWO

Scene 1

Late afternoon. About five-thirty.
AHMED enters via the gates. He's about thirty and wears
a colourful shirt and jeans. He's an elegant man, who
speaks fluent English with barely any accent. He looks
around. Sits, lights a cigarette. JILL comes from the
chalets, followed by EUNICE.

AHMED: How is she?
EUNICE: The nurse is with her now.
JILL: She's asleep.
   (JILL takes a drink. Offers it to EUNICE, who refuses.)
   So what's happening?
AHMED: We've searched everywhere ...
JILL: Oh?
AHMED: But there's no trace ... Not that I expected any.
JILL: Does this happen very often?
AHMED: What?
JILL: What happened to Sandy.
AHMED: It's never happened before.
JILL: Huh!
AHMED: I beg your pardon ...?
JILL: Surprising.
AHMED: We've never had any trouble before. Oh, the

occasional theft ... But we've never had any real
trouble before.

JILL: How long has this place been operating?

AHMED: Two years.

JILL: You ought to warn people.

AHMED: What?

JILL: Personally I shan't sleep again till I get home.
And I'm not setting foot outside here, I can tell you.

AHMED: But it's perfectly safe -

JILL: Ha!

AHMED: If you're reasonably sensible.

JILL: 'Sensible' -

AHMED: Yes.

JILL: Is that why you have all the barbed-wire and
broken glass?

AHMED: We try to protect our guests from any ...
intrusions. But we can't protect a young girl from
herself.

JILL: What? What do you mean?

AHMED: We can't protect a young girl from walking out
virtually naked if she wishes to do so.

JILL: She wasn't naked. *(Pause)* She was wrapped in a
towel from head to toe.

AHMED: *(To EUNICE)* Would you call that sensible?
(Silence) She would have been quite safe if she'd
stayed in here.

JILL: You're blaming her?

AHMED: I'm saying it was not very sensible.

JILL: *(To EUNICE)* Whenever a woman is raped there's
always some bastard who'll blame her. 'She was asking
for trouble, it was her fault, she probably wanted it
really' ... Christ!

(JILL drains her glass, refills it. ANDREW comes on.)

You feel so helpless ...

ANDREW: Martin's back.

JILL: Where is he?

ANDREW: In your chalet. I told him ...

AHMED: Were you able to speak to the girl?

ANDREW: Not really. All that I could get from her was that the boy came back and asked for a drink and she gave him one ... She stepped outside and somebody grabbed her ...

JILL: Who?

ANDREW: Somebody threw the towel over her head ...

JILL: Oh my God ...

ANDREW: I gave her a sedative. *(ANDREW takes a drink.)* All that she said was 'Arabs'.

JILL: If I could just get my hands on one of them ...

ANDREW: I know. That's how I feel.

JILL: When I think of that poor girl ...

ANDREW: Yes ...

JILL: It's the worst thing that can happen to any woman ... but a young girl like that ...

EUNICE: Where was she? Was she far away?

ANDREW: No, not very far ... but in the trees. *(Then to AHMED)* Is there anything we can do?

AHMED: What?

ANDREW: Is it worth going out again?

AHMED: There's nobody there ...

JILL: Leave it to the police.

ANDREW: Have you sent for the police?

AHMED: No.

JILL: No?

AHMED: There are so many of these beggars and vagrants who hang around the camp.

ANDREW: But you'll have to report it, Ahmed.

64

JILL: You'd better call them now. The longer you wait ...
 the less chance of catching the bastards.

AHMED: But you know what will happen –

JILL: What?

AHMED: Interrogation, publicity ...

JILL: Oh, that's it!

AHMED: What?

JILL: Are you worried about the scandal? Is that why
 you don't want to call them?

AHMED: I was thinking of the girl. She told the nurse
 not to ...

JILL: *(To ANDREW)* Did she?

ANDREW: I don't know.

AHMED: Ask the nurse. *(Pause)* I'll go and see her.

(AHMED goes off.)

JILL: Sneaky bastard!

EUNICE: Oh, Jill ...

JILL: They're all like that!

EUNICE: He's doing his best ...

JILL: Yes, his best for Number One. You can't trust
 them ... any of them. I went into the Government shop
 yesterday and there was this unctuous bastard
 serving ... He followed us round the shop, jabbering
 away and smiling like a fucking maniac ... All the
 stuff was junk so we left without buying anything. And
 as we were going out this bastard came following
 behind us with a bowl of water, sprinkling our tracks
 ... all the way out into the street!

ANDREW: I suppose he was washing away the evil spirits.

JILL: Probably.

ANDREW: What did Martin do?

JILL: Nothing. *(Pause)* They smile at you and all the time
 they hate your guts. They're corrupt. How else could

they live the way they do? I mean, I didn't exactly expect California, but ... Jesus! We went across the river in one of those little rowing boats ... wedged in with a bunch of Arabs. I was looking at the old man who was pulling the oars and I wondered where he found the strength. He was wearing a veil over his face and then the wind blew it up and I saw that half his face was eaten away. Leprosy ... but nobody bothered, nobody took any notice. They're not like us ... they take it for granted. At the jetty there was a woman sitting on the stones by the water with a baby in her arms. She was sitting on the stones with the water lapping at her feet, just staring straight ahead across the water. She was only young, a young girl in her teens ... but she looked withered. She had a begging bowl by her side. I threw a couple of dirham in ... and I looked at the baby. It was all green and pocked. I think it was dead. But the woman just sat there with her feet in the water, just staring. And nobody took any notice. They're not like us.

(Silence) I think we ought to report it.

ANDREW: What?

JILL: I think *we* ought to get the police.

ANDREW: But Ahmed said –

JILL: He just wants to avoid a scandal! And anyway I think these bastards stick together.

ANDREW: It's up to Sandy ...

JILL: But I mean ... the girl is in a state of shock. She's in no condition to know what she wants, is she?

EUNICE: *(To ANDREW)* Did you examine her?

ANDREW: Of course. *(Pause)* I took a semen swab.

JILL: Oh ...

EUNICE: Was she ... badly damaged?

ANDREW: Some scratches and abrasions, but ...

JILL: What?

ANDREW: It wasn't just rape.

JILL: What?

(Pause)

ANDREW: And it's the mental effect, the mental damage ...

JILL: Yes ... an experience like that can damage a young girl for life.

ANDREW: Yes.

JILL: A friend of mine was ... assaulted, in London. She went into her flat and there was a man in there. A thief ... but he turned on her ...

EUNICE: God ...

JILL: It may not be the same ... the same as being dragged into the trees and assaulted by Arabs ... but it was horrible for her. She was forever taking salt baths to try and wash it away. But you can't wash it out of the mind. She couldn't stand to have relations with her husband for ages ... in fact, she couldn't even go outside the door, because if a man so much as looked at her in the street she wanted to run.

ANDREW: Yes ... that's the horror of it ...

JILL: You wonder what kind of perverted, diseased minds these men have ... *(Pause)* Once or twice men have exposed themselves to me ... you know, flashing ... and I know it's nothing but it's made me feel sick ... sick, for days afterwards.

ANDREW: I suppose Sandy just wants to blank it out at the moment ... forget it ever happened.

JILL: She'll never forget it happened.

ANDREW: No, but it's a way of coping with the shame, and the guilt.

JILL: Guilt?

67

ANDREW: I don't know why it is but women do seem to feel guilty if they've been assaulted.

JILL: Because people will say she invited it. I think we ought to go and see the police ourselves.

EUNICE: But what about Sandy? Shouldn't we wait?

JILL: Wait?

EUNICE: Wait till she wakes up.

JILL: While those bastards go scot-free. *(To ANDREW)* What do you say?

ANDREW: Maybe we ought to talk to Ahmed again.

JILL: He's one of them ...

ANDREW: Let's talk to him.

(Sound of a scuffle outside. The gate is flung open. IAN comes in dragging the BOY, who holds SANDY's towel. The BOY struggles and kicks. The others stare.)

IAN: It's him! Get him.

(ANDREW leaps across to help.)

He had the towel ...

ANDREW: Where was he?

IAN: In the trees ... get hold of him!

(The BOY struggles wildly. ANDREW pulls the towel from him. The BOY kicks IAN.)

Bastard!

(IAN wrestles with the BOY, they slip and fall to the ground, IAN swearing and the BOY shouting in Arabic. ANDREW stands over them, trying to grab the BOY as they roll about. IAN manages to pin the BOY to the ground ... the BOY rips his nails down IAN's face and scrambles free and runs towards the gates. He's confronted by JILL. ANDREW leaps after him. IAN lies holding his face.)

Fucking bastard!

(The BOY turns and tries to escape across the garden.

ANDREW trips him and he falls sprawling. ANDREW jumps after him and drags him up.)

ANDREW: What happened? What happened to the girl?

(The BOY is panic-stricken and shouts in Arabic.)

Was it you?

(ANDREW slaps him hard ... the BOY reels back and ANDREW follows up.)

Was it you? Who was it? Who was it?

EUNICE: Andrew!

(The BOY spits in ANDREW's face and slips free. IAN bars the way. The BOY seizes a bottle.)

IAN: Come here ...

(The BOY holds up the bottle threateningly.)

JILL: Ian!

IAN: Bastard!

(IAN closes on the BOY. ANDREW follows. The BOY backs against the wall, holding the bottle high in warning. He is surrounded by ANDREW, IAN and JILL. EUNICE is standing back.)

JILL: He's the one ...

ANDREW: What happened? What happened with the girl?

EUNICE: Andrew ... wait ...

(EUNICE tries to intervene but ANDREW throws her back.)

ANDREW: Get back!

(IAN makes a grab for the bottle and the BOY hits him on the head with it. As he does so ANDREW grabs his arm and pulls him away, then twists his arm to get the bottle. The BOY kicks and struggles desperately. Finally, ANDREW forces the bottle out of his grasp, hits him on the side of the head. The BOY falls back. ANDREW goes after him.)

IAN: Kill the bastard!

(The BOY half runs and half falls backwards as ANDREW

pursues him, shouting wildly.)

ANDREW: Was it you? Filthy little bastard! Was it you?
(The BOY lifts his arms to protect himself. ANDREW brings the bottle down on them, and then, berserk, smashes the bottle down on his head and face, screaming at him.)

EUNICE: Stop it, stop it!
(MARTIN comes on. Wears a white linen suit.)

MARTIN: What -
(EUNICE flies to him.)

EUNICE: Martin, stop them!

MARTIN: What's going on?
(The BOY collapses. MARTIN runs across and pushes the others aside. Looks down at the BOY, who is bleeding badly.)

IAN: It's him ...

MARTIN: What the hell ... *(MARTIN looks at ANDREW, then kneels down to the BOY.)* Oh my God ... What have you done? *(MARTIN lifts the BOY up.)* What have you done?
(MARTIN carries the BOY off.

IAN looks at JILL.

EUNICE stares at ANDREW, who stands transfixed, the bottle dangling from his hand. His eyes are blank and he seems in a state of total shock.)

BLACKOUT

(MUSIC)

Scene 2

Early evening. Lamps glowing in the trees. JILL and ANDREW.

JILL wears a dramatic black dress. ANDREW, sports jacket and flannels. MARTIN comes on, wearing the bloodstained suit.

MARTIN: Ahmed is livid. Absolutely livid. He's out for your blood. He's agreed to listen to Sandy, but ... where is she?

ANDREW: Eunice is bringing her.

MARTIN: He's determined to call the police.

JILL: The police?

MARTIN: Of course. What d'you expect?

JILL: He didn't want to call the police about Sandy. The bastard ...

MARTIN: You'd better be nice to him.

JILL: What?

MARTIN: He's no fool. Don't underestimate him. I'm as sure as dammit that he was involved in the coup here... the attempted coup. You know he's a trained pilot? He served six years in the RAF. Don't underestimate Ahmed. You may need him.

JILL: I may?

MARTIN: You all may.

JILL: But not you ...

MARTIN: I wasn't here.

JILL: No ... No, you weren't here. Where were you?

MARTIN: You know where I was.

JILL: Where?

MARTIN: In the town.

JILL: Sipping mint tea with your bumboys?

MARTIN: Doing my bit for Anglo-Arab relations.

JILL: Ha!

(Silence)

MARTIN: *(Angry)* What on earth possessed you?

JILL: Look, Martin ... You must understand —

MARTIN: It doesn't matter whether I understand. Do you think the police will?

JILL: I mean you must understand how we felt about Sandy. If you'd been there ... when Andrew carried her in ...

MARTIN: But to attack the boy ... Honestly, you must have been fucking mad!

JILL: You would have done the same!

MARTIN: Would I?

(AHMED comes on.)

Oh, Ahmed ... we've been talking about the boy. Seems he'll be all right after all. *(To ANDREW)* Won't he?

ANDREW: After a few days in bed. A few days nursing.

MARTIN: Yes, so I was saying that ... if it's a question of money, I'm sure we can raise quite a bit between us. I mean, if we all chip in ... we can cover the cost of his accommodation here and food and all that. Something for the nurse, of course ... and for your trouble. *(Pause)* In a few days he'll be right as rain. Tough little buggers, these boys! D'you know his family?

AHMED: He doesn't have any family.

MARTIN: Oh ...

AHMED: He's one of my boys.

(Pause. MARTIN stares.)

MARTIN: 'Your' boys?

AHMED: He earns a few dirhams doing odd jobs for me. Running errands to town. It's all he has.

MARTIN: Oh, I see. Well, if we could just keep him in
bed for a few days ... I mean, no need to broadcast
it ...

AHMED: That's out of the question.

MARTIN: What?

AHMED: Do you really think we can keep him in a chalet
here without people talking? The nurse and the cook
and the gardener and ... the guests? The other
guests? You can't buy them all.

MARTIN: But let's be realistic -

AHMED: *(Angry)* D'you think he would have come anywhere
near here if he had been involved in the attack on the
girl?

JILL: But he had her towel -

AHMED: He found the towel -

JILL: He was there. Sandy told Andrew.

ANDREW: What she said was -

JILL: And anyway ... we only wanted to talk to him but he
went berserk.

AHMED: You probably terrified him.

JILL: If he was so innocent, why wouldn't he talk to us?

AHMED: For one thing he can't speak English. *(Silence)*
I'll have to report it.

MARTIN: Ahmed.

(AHMED looks at MARTIN. Pause.)

Let's be realistic ...

AHMED: 'Realistic'?

MARTIN: You must understand how these people felt about
Sandy. Of course that may not justify what happened
to the boy, but ... but think what will happen if you
report this. We'll all be detained here, guilty or
innocent, until they've made their enquiries or even
until the trial. God knows how long that will be. And

73

of course, the whole story about Sandy will have to
come out. It's the only excuse for ... what happened
afterwards. She'll have to endure all that humiliating
business of interrogation and examination ... and of
course the whole thing will be splashed across the
English newspapers. It's the sort of story they love.
Think of the publicity you'll get. I mean, you might
as well close this place up here and now. Think about
it.

AHMED: Perhaps we should.

MARTIN: What?

AHMED: Close this place up.

MARTIN: Before you make your decision, I suggest you at least inform the owners.

AHMED: The owners are in Surrey.

(Silence)

MARTIN: Think of your own position.

AHMED: What?

MARTIN: You've got a good number here. You don't want to throw it away for nothing.

AHMED: For nothing?

MARTIN: What will you gain?

(EUNICE comes on with SANDY. EUNICE wears a print dress, SANDY a long skirt and top.
JILL jumps up and runs over to SANDY.)

JILL: Sandy ... darling ...

(JILL hugs her. SANDY sits in a chair. JILL sits with MARTIN, and EUNICE with ANDREW. There is almost a suggestion of a trial here.)

AHMED: How are you?

SANDY: All right, thanks.

MARTIN: Would you like a drink?

SANDY: Thanks.

(MARTIN gives SANDY a glass of red wine.)

AHMED: I know it must be ... distressing for you, but if you can ... We were hoping you could tell us what happened. *(Pause)* Do you feel up to talking?

SANDY: Yes.

AHMED: You were here ... alone ...

SANDY: Yes.

AHMED: Sunbathing.

SANDY: I had the bath towel wrapped around me.

AHMED: Yes ...

SANDY: And ... I saw the boy.

AHMED: Where was he?

SANDY: Outside. By the gates.

AHMED: The gates were open?

SANDY: Yes.

MARTIN: I'd opened them earlier on to give the boy a drink.

AHMED: I see.

SANDY: So I gave him a drink.

AHMED: Did he come in?

SANDY: No ... I stepped outside.

JILL: He wanted you to ...

SANDY: I think he was nervous.

AHMED: So you stepped outside and gave him a drink?

SANDY: Yes.

AHMED: Did you see anybody?

SANDY: No ... only the boy. He said, 'Thank you'. And then ... it was very hot, and quiet ... I could hear the tide ... and I remember looking through the trees at the minaret. I walked along to get a better view ...

AHMED: Was the boy with you?

SANDY: No.

AHMED: Where was he?

SANDY: I don't know.

AHMED: So you walked along ...

SANDY: Yes ... not very far, just a few yards ... and then somebody grabbed my towel and threw it over my head -

JILL: But did you see who it was?

SANDY: Not then.

JILL: But where could they have come from?

SANDY: I suppose they were in the trees ...

AHMED: Go on ...

SANDY: They grabbed hold of me and took me to where Andrew found me.

JILL: Oh God ...

MARTIN: 'They'?

SANDY: There were two of them.

JILL: You must have been ... terrified!

SANDY: It all happened so quickly. At first I thought it was somebody playing a prank ... I mean, when it happened. But then ... the towel was clamped over my mouth and I was lifted off my feet and my arms were trapped. They carried me through the trees and put me down ... I was on my face, then I was turned onto my back ... and then the men pulled the towel away and I saw them.

AHMED: Would you recognize them?

JILL: What were they like?

SANDY: They were both young. One was short and stocky with dark skin ... and the other was tall, with that kind of lighter skin ... light brown, like Ahmed. The tall one was kneeling over me and holding me down by the shoulders. I tried to scream but the other man put his hand over my mouth. I could hardly breathe. And I tried to kick and struggle ... but I couldn't move ... I just panicked completely ... *(Pause)* Then the man who was kneeling on me ... he took away the other man's hand so I was able to breathe ... and he started saying something, whispering to me ...

JILL: What was he saying?

SANDY: It was in Arabic. And I tried to scream, but I couldn't ... I was in such a state of panic that my mouth opened and my lips moved but there was no sound coming out, like in a dream ... and all the time the man was talking. And then he put his hand on my throat. I thought I was going to die. I started kicking out, kicking madly ... and the other man got hold of my legs ... I was completely helpless.

JILL: God ...

SANDY: And then I begged them ... and the man was looking at me and he put his hand on my mouth ... just touched it for a second. He was still holding my throat ... and I realized it was a warning, he was telling me they didn't want to kill me but they would kill me if ... if they had to. I just ... collapsed inside, I went completely limp, I just lay there ...

MARTIN: That was sensible ...

SANDY: No, it wasn't.

MARTIN: What?

SANDY: It was purely instinctive ... an animal instinct. Inside I was melting ... I was shaking with fear. I couldn't resist.

(Silence)

JILL: And then?

(Silence)

SANDY: The dark man had hold of my arms, pinning me down ... And the other man ... I couldn't resist, I knew it was hopeless, but inside I was screaming, I was thinking, My God is this happening, this is actually happening to

me, this nightmare is real ... I shut my eyes. The
man was stroking my hair and fondling me and I was
lying frozen. And he began kissing ... kissing and
biting ... I mean he kissed me on the face and ... all
over the body ... and then, there ... And I began to
cry ... I began crying desperately and begging them to
let me go and the other man sat on my face and I was
smothering and gasping for air. He was squeezing my
breasts and ...

JILL: Uggh ...

SANDY: The pain was atrocious. I felt mangled. *(Silence)* I couldn't resist.

MARTIN: No ... no.

SANDY: I mean, I was resisting. I was resisting, but only inside. I couldn't resist physically, they were too powerful. And then suddenly the man slipped off me and grabbed hold of my hair and yanked it up - the pain shot through my head and he forced me up - and they turned me round and made me kneel ... like a dog ...

JILL: Oh my God ...

SANDY: The dark man crushed me into him ... he had his arms round my body and was gripping my breasts and he forced me to ... to suck him. And the other man ...

JILL: Animals!

MARTIN: All right. All right.

SANDY: The other man buggered me.

MARTIN: All right ... drink this.

(MARTIN refills SANDY's glass and she drinks.)

JILL: *(To AHMED)* Satisfied?

MARTIN: Jill!

(MARTIN gives JILL a drink. IAN comes on.)

IAN: Andrew - the nurse wants you.

ANDREW: What?

IAN: It's the boy. He's bleeding.

ANDREW: Bleeding?

IAN: She wants you now.

(ANDREW goes off.)

SANDY: The boy?

AHMED: Didn't you know?

SANDY: What?

AHMED: They battered him.

SANDY: Battered him? Who?

(AHMED gestures around the group.)

AHMED: I'll have to report it to the police.

SANDY: The police?

AHMED: Yes - don't you want them?

SANDY: I wouldn't report a rape back home. I certainly don't want to report it here.

AHMED: You'll get justice.

(AHMED goes off.)

MARTIN: Ahmed - wait. Hang on! *(MARTIN follows AHMED.)* There'll be one hell of a scandal. All hell will be let loose if -

(MARTIN goes off.)

SANDY: What happened to the boy?

JILL: He came back here. There was a fight. Andrew hit him with a bottle.

SANDY: Andrew did?

EUNICE: It wasn't just Andrew. It was all of us. We were all involved.

SANDY: But I don't understand -

JILL: For Christ's sake, you told Andrew you went out to give him a drink and somebody jumped you, didn't you?

SANDY: Yes, but -

JILL: You must realize how we felt about you.

79

SANDY: But why batter him?

JILL: Oh, for Christ's sake, Sandy! It's all very well for you to sit there looking shocked. You can give your evidence and go home and tell your party piece. But what do you think is going to happen to us? To the rest of us? We only did it because of you.

SANDY: Me?

JILL: Yes.

SANDY: You battered him because of me?

JILL: Yes.

SANDY: But even if he had been involved —

JILL: Which he was!

SANDY: He wasn't!

JILL: I'd kill any monster who'd attack a woman.

SANDY: That's insane!

JILL: Look, they probably sent him in deliberately —

SANDY: Who?

JILL: The men who were hiding in the trees.

SANDY: I don't know if they were hiding.

JILL: What?

SANDY: I don't know whether they just happened to see me ...

JILL: You mean they just happened to be there when you came out? I don't believe it. I think they were using the boy as a decoy. And anyway — he must have seen them. He must have seen them!

IAN: We only wanted to ask him about you but he went berserk.

(Silence)

JILL: You'd better think about what you're going to say to the police. From what you've told us ... I doubt if they'll be much more sympathetic to you than to the rest of us.

SANDY: Me?

JILL: Yes, you.

SANDY: Why me?

JILL: Oh, come on, Sandy!

SANDY: What?

JILL: You're the main cause of the whole damn thing. If you hadn't gone marching out of here, nothing would have happened.

SANDY: But I only stepped outside ... a little way.

JILL: It's not a question of how far you stepped. It's a question of in-here or out-there! Ahmed is quite right.

EUNICE: Oh Jill ...

JILL: It's true! It *was* crazy to go out like that. And wrapped in a towel! You were asking for it. You wouldn't go marching through Hyde Park wrapped in a towel, would you? If it hadn't been for you nothing would have happened. You'll have a job explaining your behaviour to the police. You could at least say he was with them. At least it makes more sense ...

SANDY: I don't think he was involved.

JILL: You don't think he was involved? You don't *think*. *(To the others)* What do you think?

EUNICE: I think we'll just have to tell the truth.

JILL: 'The truth' will incarcerate us all.

EUNICE: But if we say it was an accident –

(Silence)

JILL: Christ, this is crazy! *(JILL looks at SANDY.)* We're all going to end up in prison. And she's sitting there like a cat who's had the cream!

EUNICE: Jill!

SANDY: What do you want me to do?

JILL: I want you to save us.

81

SANDY: Save you?

JILL: Yes.

SANDY: How?

JILL: Scream and weep and tear your hair out. Show them you've been *raped*, for God's sake!

SANDY: Look, I'm in one piece.

JILL: Ha!

SANDY: I'm in one piece. I'm alive, I'm not damaged.

JILL: You're not damaged?

SANDY: No, I'm not damaged! Do you wish I was?

JILL: You didn't resist ...

SANDY: What?

JILL: You didn't put up much resistance, did you?

SANDY: That doesn't mean I consented.

EUNICE: If she had resisted she might have been strangled.

JILL: Oh, what do you know?

EUNICE: What?

JILL: What do you know about sex? You haven't a clue what's going on.

EUNICE: What do you mean?

JILL: *(To SANDY)* Not damaged? Gang-banged, and not damaged?

SANDY: It's over. It's over.

JILL: Is it?

SANDY: Look, I'm on the pill, there'll be no consequences. It's over.

JILL: Oh, you're so modern –

SANDY: What do you want me to do? Hide myself, or slit my throat?

(JILL stares at SANDY.)

JILL: Jesus! It wouldn't surprise me to hear she had a fucking climax!

EUNICE: Jill!

(SANDY breaks down, crying. EUNICE holds her.
ANDREW comes on.)

ANDREW: He's dead. Haemorrhage.

JILL: Haemorrhage?

ANDREW: Yes.

JILL: But ... couldn't you tell ...

ANDREW: No. There was no way of knowing. He just haemorrhaged. We couldn't tell.

JILL: And he's dead ...

ANDREW: Yes.

JILL: Oh Christ! Well, that is it! That's all we need! That is it!

EUNICE: Shut up, Jill.

JILL: I'm fucked if I'm going to spend the rest of my life in an Arab gaol for the sake of that little cow! *(Hysterical)* Look at her. Sitting there. All innocent. She marched out of here half-naked and got gang-banged ... and she tells it straight like a story out of True Romances! Jesus! I won't have it! I won't have it! The cow!

EUNICE: DAMN WELL SHUT UP!

(EUNICE clips JILL on the cheek. JILL sinks down, shuddering, crying. IAN puts his arm around her. She shrugs it off.)

ANDREW: Don't worry ...

EUNICE: What?

ANDREW: I was to blame.

EUNICE: What do you mean?

ANDREW: I killed him.

EUNICE: But it was an accident.

ANDREW: Was it?

EUNICE: You didn't mean to kill him.

ANDREW: Didn't I?

EUNICE: No.

ANDREW: I wanted to batter him. I'll talk to the police.

IAN: What'll you say?

ANDREW: I'll say I found the boy in here, and there was a fight -

SANDY: No.

ANDREW: What?

SANDY: You can't do that.

ANDREW: Why not?

SANDY: But they'll never understand ...

(Silence)

JILL: Let's see what Martin has to say.

IAN: Where is he?

ANDREW: He's talking to Ahmed.

EUNICE: You know ...

SANDY: What?

EUNICE: I think Andrew is right.

SANDY: Right?

EUNICE: I think he is to blame.

SANDY: What?

EUNICE: After all he did kill the boy.

ANDREW: I said I did.

EUNICE: And we know why he did.

(Pause)

JILL: *(Icy)* Oh my God ...

(MARTIN comes on.)

EUNICE: And now he wants to play the martyr.

MARTIN: Actually we don't need a martyr.

JILL: What?

MARTIN: Ahmed has agreed to co-operate.

JILL: You've bribed him.

MARTIN: Of course. He's making arrangements for us to fly home tomorrow.

JILL: All of us?

MARTIN: Of course.

JILL: How much?

MARTIN: Seven hundred and fifty.

JILL: What, pounds?

MARTIN: What do you think? Dirhams? Anyway, he wanted a thousand but I beat him down.

JILL: Christ, what a fucking hypocrite!

MARTIN: What?

JILL: The way he carried on about the boy earlier! Said he couldn't look after him.

MARTIN: No, he's right.

JILL: Why?

MARTIN: It's easier now ...

JILL: What do you mean?

MARTIN: Ahmed says it's easier now the boy is dead.

JILL: What's he going to do about the boy?

MARTIN: Bury him.

(Pause)

SANDY: But we can't do that!

MARTIN: What do you want to do? Stay here? Be realistic. The boy is dead, you're alive. How much have we got?
(JILL looks in her handbag, takes out cash, gives it to MARTIN.)

JILL: Over two hundred.

MARTIN: Good.
(MARTIN counts the money. EUNICE checks her handbag, IAN his wallet. They kneel together on the grass to count.)
That's two hundred and twenty quid in all. Ian ... how about you?

IAN: I've got forty quid in sterling, sixty in travellers' cheques, and about four hundred dirhams.

JILL: That's about a hundred and thirty-five quid.

MARTIN: Is it? Right.

(MARTIN puts the amounts together in stacks of sterling, travellers' cheques and dirhams.)

What's that make?

JILL: Three hundred and thirty-five.

MARTIN: Good.

(EUNICE hands over her money.)

EUNICE: There's one hundred and eighty in travellers' cheques, thirty pounds and about six hundred dirhams.

JILL: Two hundred and sixty.

MARTIN: Two hundred and sixty on top of three hundred and —

JILL: Six hundred and fifteen.

MARTIN: Bit short.

SANDY: How much did he want?

MARTIN: Seven hundred and fifty.

SANDY: I've got over a hundred in the chalet.

MARTIN: Oh, no ... We can't ask you.

SANDY: Don't be ridiculous.

JILL: Then that's seven hundred and fifteen.

MARTIN: I've got twenty quid here.

JILL: Seven hundred and thirty-five ...

MARTIN: We'll have to walk home from Heathrow.

(AHMED comes on. They all stop and look at him.)

We're just sorting things out ...

AHMED: The flights are arranged for tomorrow afternoon.

MARTIN: Oh, good.

AHMED: I'll lay on transport to the airport in the morning.

MARTIN: Thanks.

AHMED: You'd better cash these travellers' cheques in the morning.

MARTIN: Yes ... we'll do that.

AHMED: The tours will be back in an hour or so.

MARTIN: Yes, well ... we'll make ourselves scarce.

AHMED: If you do come back to Morocco, perhaps you might remember that we have a different culture to yours.

JILL: We had noticed.

AHMED: Wait for a few years, and then you'll probably find it more congenial here.

JILL: What?

AHMED: In a few years our women will probably be bathing on the beach, and the Casbah will be replaced by a block of hotels, and the Medina by a supermarket ... and you'll probably be much happier here then.

JILL: Do you think any of us would come back here?

AHMED: No. But I expect that by then we'll be spending our holidays with you ... In fact, by then you'll probably be learning Arabic.

(AHMED goes off.)

JILL: Sanctimonious bastard!

IAN: Isn't he?

JILL: Seven hundred and fifty quid and a fucking lecture too!

MARTIN: We haven't got the seven hundred and fifty yet.

JILL: We'll have to give him our contraband.

EUNICE: *(To ANDREW)* Give me your wallet.

(ANDREW passes EUNICE his wallet.)

There's about twenty-five here.

(EUNICE gives the notes to MARTIN.)

MARTIN: Oh, well, that's it. That's virtually it.

JILL: That's more than it.

MARTIN: Is it?

JILL: You can give her ten back.

MARTIN: Oh ...

(MARTIN returns ten pounds to EUNICE.)

Remember we've got to cash these cheques in the morning.

>   Ahmed only deals in cash.
>
> EUNICE: We'll pay it all back.
>
> MARTIN: What?
>
> EUNICE: We'll pay you back when we get home.
>
> MARTIN: Rubbish! Let's check this.
>
>   *(MARTIN begins a final check on the money. A jet is heard in the distance. JILL looks up in the direction of the plane.)*
>
>   Ten pounds ... twenty pounds ... thirty ...
>
> JILL: Boy ... Will I be glad to get back to civilization!
>
>   *(The sound of the jet increases in volume. As they kneel around the money, all look up at the plane passing directly overhead. The sound reaches deafening proportions.)*
>
>   BLACKOUT